DRAG RACING

BILL HOLDER

Photography by BOB FAIRMAN
Foreword by EDDIE HILL
First Four-Second Drag Racer

BISON GROUP

DRAG RACING

Contents

First published in 1993 by
Bison Books Ltd.
Kimbolton House
117A Fulham Road
London SW3 6RL

ISBN 1-85841-005-3

Printed in Hong Kong

Foreword

If someone had told me when I was a kid that one day I'd be driving a 25-foot-long missile made of magnesium and chrome-moly tubing powered by a 5000-horsepower engine running on rocket propellant (nitromethane), I would never have believed it. When I built my first dragster, I had never seen one before, except in a new magazine called *Hot Rod*. When I won my first race in that dragster, I knew I was hooked for life.

Hooked is right. I've spent four and a half decades on the cutting edge of elapsed time and mph in cars, boats, and on motorcycles. The thrill of speed and the rush of adrenaline has kept me coming back for more, decade after decade, win or lose, setting records or flipping over backwards. Danger is the price of racing, yet every racer will tell you he's looking forward to his next lap.

It's been a long time since I was a kid with my copies of racing magazines, dreaming of being one of the fast guys. I guess I finally got there, and that's where I hope to stay until I'm too old to crawl into the cockpit.

Eddie Hill

Eddie Hill
First Four-Second Drag Racer

Page 1: *For many fans, the most exciting aspect of drag racing occurs before the car ever gets to the starting line. The burnout, during which the rear tires are superheated for traction purposes, is the most spectacular part of the sport.*

Foldout: *This unique Top Alcohol Dragster, which sports two fuel-injected engines, is able to perform one of the most spectacular burnouts in drag racing today.*

Roots

The sights, sounds, and smells of drag racing – there's nothing else like them in the world of motorsports. All the senses are encompassed in this battle of one-on-one.

The firing of a 4000-horsepower nitromethane-burning engine literally shakes the ground with a roaring thunder. A California earthquake has nothing on one of these machines. Then, there's the drama of a pair of superwide racing slicks being spun up to speed, torching against the pavement and raising a huge acrid cloud of smoke as the tires are heated for their appointed mission. It might be a smelly cloud to the un-initiated, but to the millions of drag racing fans around the world, it's the sweet smell of power and performance.

Born in the United States, drag racing comprises a lot more than the professional big leagues of the sport that get all the national TV coverage. For many, the sport is a family activity with both young and old, male and female, actively partici-pating. Some families are in their second, and even third, generation in the sport.

Right: The fastest machines in drag racing are the 300-inch wheelbase, nitromethane-burning Top Fuel dragsters. This Top Fueler heats its tires with a monstrous burnout.

Below: Up-and-comer Scott Geoffrion prepares his Pro Stock dragster for a race by laying down a patch of rubber to aid in traction off the line.

Unlike any other motorsport in the United States, drag racing is more of a participant sport than an observer sport. In what other sport can you put the family sedan directly into competition on the track? Involvement in the sport begins this way for many enthusiasts, but a quest for more speed often results in the building of higher performance machines.

Drag racing is also increasingly popular in Europe and Australia. A number of foreign drivers have participated in national competitions in the US. Currently, there are also two events with the American circuits held in Canada.

Admittedly, not all drag racing is done at an authorized facility. An unlawful version of the sport is carried out from stoplight to stoplight to prove the performance of one's car. The movement toward organized drag racing in the US and elsewhere has greatly reduced the dangerous undertaking of unauthorized racing.

Drag racing as we know it began on dry lake beds in California following World War II. The fledgling sport was first organized by the Southern California Timing Association, which consisted of some two dozen clubs. The organization sanctioned events at Muroc Dry Lake and other locations in the area.

The National Hot Rod Association (NHRA) came into existence in 1951 and set the direction of the drag sport for the future. The initial races held by the NHRA, under Wally Parks, were called regionals and were held at various locations across the United States.

The creation of the NHRA occurred at a time when drag racing was exploding across the country, much of it taking place in Saturday night duels at stoplights. The NHRA sought to address that dangerous avocation and move the activity to the supervised drag strip. Interestingly, many of these early drag facilities were old military air base runways.

The NHRA strived hard to spread the word on the sport, and set standards with particular emphasis on safety. It continues in that direction in the 1990s.

Like other motorsports activities, other sanctioning bodies would be created to challenge the kingpin organization. One group that came on the scene when the NHRA decided to disallow the use of the powerful nitromethane fuel in the 1960s was the American Hot Rod Association (AHRA). This organization really set a foothold when it reorganized the wild and crazy nitro-fueled 'funny cars' as a separate class.

Left: *The exciting Top Alcohol Funny Cars are just fractions of a second slower than their nitro-powered Funny Car big brothers.*

Above: *A Super Gas dragster lights up its tires in the burnout area.*

Below: *The rail dragster design is over four decades old. This machine,* The Bug, *was built and driven by Dick Kraft in the late 1940s and early 1950s.*

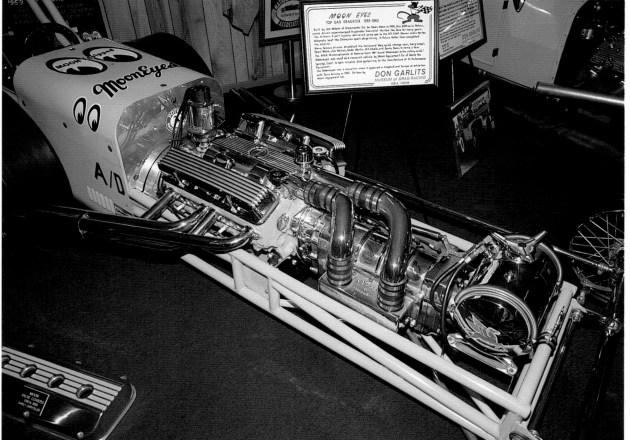

Above: *This is the first of the many* Swamp Rat *machines built and driven by Don Garlits. Driven in the late 1950s, the car was capable of 180 mile per hour speeds.*

Left: *This late-1950s Top Gas dragster,* Moon Eyes, *was powered by a supercharged V-8 Chevy motor.*

Far left: *In the early 1980s, Don Garlits experimented with a traverse-mounted blown 454 Hemi engine in a dragster called the* Sidewinder.

Far left: *In its day, the classic 1957 Chevy was popular at the drag strip as well as on the street. Funny Car veteran Tom 'The Mongoose' McEwen drove a Funny Car version at strips across the country. This is a recreation of that famous car.*

Two other groups came on board in the 1970s when legend Don Garlits formed the now-defunct Professional Racers Association, and the International Hot Rod Association (IHRA) was formed. The IHRA continues to be a major force in national drag racing in the 1990s.

Drag racing as an organized sport took off in the early 1960s with the involvement of the car companies which suddenly realized that the exposure of drag racing, like NASCAR competition, could help sell cars from the showroom floor.

The class that showcased these modified production cars was called Super Stock, and the competition was fierce. Chevy brought its awesome 409 cubic-inch engine to the strip. Pontiac showed up with a hot tri-carbureted 389 cubic-inch powerhouse, while Chrysler showed its stuff with a ground-pounding 413 cubic-inch engine under the hood. Ford came back with its awesome 406 triple-carbed response.

The production models of those machines carried those magic numbers proudly on their front flanks. When a national win was recorded, the exploit was reported in the national press and used in the winning company's advertising campaign, and many cars were sold. The competition between car manufacturers was pursued on hundreds of local drag strips across the country, resulting in lots of excitement for the fans and thriving business for the manufacturers. In fact, more than one young driver bought one of those big block machines right off the showroom floor and took it directly to the drag strip!

But the companies did more than just build high-powered production machines. They also authorized and built limited numbers of pure racecars. One of the most famous of such machines was the Ford Thunderbolt, of which only about 100 were built. Constructed just for drag racing, the cars couldn't be driven legally on the street.

The Thunderbolt featured an aluminum front end with ram-air ducting from the headlight holes. With a 425 horsepower powerhouse engine under the hood and a weight of only 3200 pounds, the cars could turn a 12-second quarter-mile performance. Famous drivers such as Butch Leal, Hubert Platt, Gas Ronda, and Phil Bonner drove the Thunderbolts with great success. There was also a similar drag car version of the Mercury known as the A/FX Comet.

The car companies also produced models with less vigorous factory modifications. Known as 'lightweights,' these low production models also carried lightweight front ends for improved performance at the drag strips.

One such model was the 1962/63 Pontiac Super Duty 421 Catalina. The lightweight option with this model used aluminum for the inner and outer fenders, hood, nosepiece, valance, and front and rear bumpers. In addition, there was no radio or heater. This was as close as you could get to a racecar right off the showroom floor.

The other manufacturers had similar offerings. Ford produced a lightweight version of its Galaxie in the early 1960s, while Chevy 'lightened up' some of its 409 cubic-inch-powered Impalas. In 1968, Chrysler built 80 specially prepared Hemi-powered lightweight Dodge Darts for drag use only. And there were other examples. This was factory drag racing in its finest hour.

Far left above: *This early 1960s Plymouth Belvedere altered-wheelbase car was a forerunner of the popular Super Stock Class. This original car is still involved in bracket racing today.*

Far left below: *The use of 1960s cars is still popular in racing in the 1990s. Here a vintage Dodge station wagon, hauling gas instead of groceries, gets off the line at Tri-State Dragway near Hamilton, Ohio.*

Above: *Early modified Chrysler-powered street cars were big winners at the nation's drag strips. Sox & Martin was a predominant team. Here, a replica of a 1970 Superbird represents that glorious drag racing era.*

Right: *With British sheet metal on the outside and American V-8 power under the hood, these Anglias are a popular entry in the NHRA Super Gas Class.*

The Super Stock Class kept evolving, with the cars getting faster and faster. As a result, toward the end of the decade, the Pro Stock Class was added. These early days of Pro Stock brought kingpins such as Don Carlton in the famous Motown Missile, Grumpy Jenkins, the legendary Sox & Martin team, 'Dyno' Don Nicholson, and Don Landy to the strip.

As Pro Stock moved into the late 1970s, new names came into play, with Ford driver Bob Glidden at the top. This popular class has since matured, and performance has moved from the ten-second runs of the 1970s to screaming seven-second jaunts in the 1990s. The 'factory racers' have come of age.

Those great old days still live on in today's drag racing scene. At drag strips across the country, dragsters carrying those old 1950s and 1960s bodies, or fiberglass replicas of them, can be seen doing what is referred to as nostalgic racing.

In addition to the Pro Stock Class, during the late 1960s the Funny Car Class was also born. These cars achieved immediate popularity with their nitro-burning high performance. The makers of these machines also were starting to utilize fiberglass bodies and exotic powerplants. With all their parts custom-made, the only thing stock about these machines is their appearance.

Many of these high-technology machines were capable even back then of seven- to eight-second quarter-mile performance. Don 'The Snake' Prudhomme and 'Ohio George' Montgomery were two of the leaders in the Funny Car revolution.

Stock-appearing dragsters had their place, but other builders liked to make their machines in the shape of a long sleek-nosed arrow. The leader and innovator in this class in the beginning, and for decades to follow, was 'Big Daddy' Don Garlits. Don built the first example of what would eventually become the Top Fuel Class car as we know it today. In 1954, though, it was still a fledgling class, with one of Garlits's early machines using a vintage Ford flathead engine.

A revolution took place in this class when Garlits built his first rear engine Top Fueler in 1970. The advanced machine would win six national events. Over the years, Garlits would built a whole series of 'Swamp Rat' racers, each on the cutting edge of technology.

The stars of the 1970s and 1980s Top Fuel ranks included Shirley — they called her 'Cha Cha' at the time — Muldowney, whose pink Top Fuel machines won three national NHRA titles. Another superstar of the time who remains active in the 1990s was the always innovative Connie Kalitta.

The big three classes got most of the attention in the national press, but it was still a small part of the sport in those days. Drag racing at the amateur level was growing tremendously, with thousands of cars showing up at hundreds of strips. Even motorcycle dragsters were appearing in surprising numbers.

Left: *Weight-saving was a consideration in drag racing even in the 1950s. Note the holes drilled in the front axle of this dragster. Also note the leaf springs, the mounting angle of the shocks, and the absence of front brakes.*

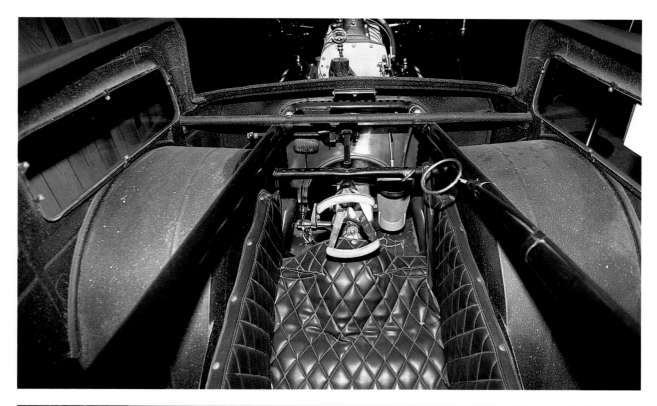

Left: *The cockpit of this 1960s Altered Fuel Coupe has a 'go' pedal on the right and a 'stop' pedal on the left. The ring on the roll cage, when pulled, activated the parachute which assisted in slowing the car.*

Left below: *Three famous early Funny Cars are displayed at the Don Garlits Museum of Drag Racing in Ocala, Florida. Left to right, the cars are Raymond Beadle's* Blue Max, *Candies and Hughes'* Old Milwaukee, *and Don 'The Snake' Prudhomme's* Skoal Bandit.

Far left: *This early rail-frame dragster owner added a touch of class with whitewalls on his racing slicks. Power for this vintage machine came from a Ford flathead V-8 with four one-barrel carburetors. It was state-of-the-art in the 1950s. How times have changed!*

Below: *In the early 1970s, most sponsors involved with drag racing were connected to the automotive industry in some way. Don Prudhomme's sponsor, Mattel Toys, was the maker of Hot Wheels miniature cars for children.*

Below center: *Shirley Muldowney was a major force in NHRA Top Fuel racing during the 1980s, when she won three national championships. This is her 1980 Attebury car painted in her familiar pink color.*

Currently, there are approximately 250 active drag strips in the United States, 22 in Canada, and one in Mexico. In Great Britain, there are three active drag strips and as many as 300 competitors. Interest also continues to grow in Japan, Australia, Sweden, and in Germany, where the drag sport was introduced by American GIs.

In the US, the NHRA alone has a membership of over 80,000 and some 23,000 drivers. And there were over a half-million local bracket racers in 1991. For the 1990s, a massive new drag facility is planned for a location north of Dayton, Ohio, with a 30,000-seat capacity. It's a vivid indication of the growing interest in the sport.

There are also drag activities in other realms, with active programs which have grown through the years, in sand dragging, mud drags and boat drags. Even the popular monster trucks have drag races against each other.

The sport of drag racing, with its humble beginnings, has come of age big time in the 1990s. One can but wonder what the coming years will hold.

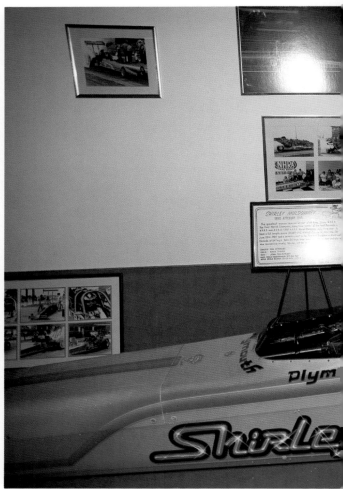

Left: *Removal of the body panels on a Garlits Top Fuel dragster reveals attention to detail as well as the safety concerns for the driver. A super-strong chrome-moly cage encircling the driver has helped many to survive potentially catastrophic crashes.*

Below: *Early attempts at streamlining produced this unusual tail fin configuration. The wild paint scheme surely must have made it a fan favorite, regardless of how well it did.*

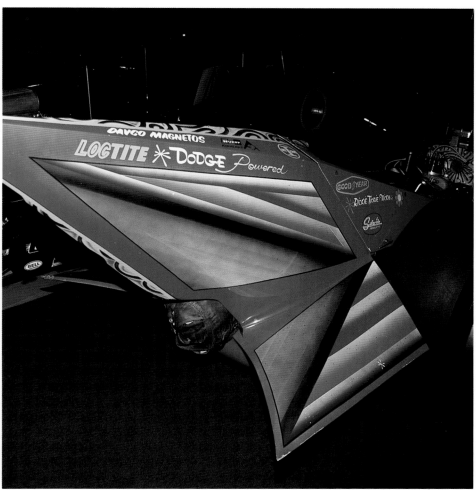

23

Right: *This aerial view of the NHRA US Nationals shows the standard dragstrip layout: the starting line, the Christmas Tree, the center lane divider and the outside retaining wall. Here, two Top Fuel dragsters are seen leaving the starting line, leaving a trail of clutch dust.*

Far right: *Large signs at the finish line instantaneously identify the winner. In this image, the Top Fuel dragster in the Winston Lane has run a 4.91-second elapsed time with a top speed of 295.56 miles per hour.*

The principles of drag racing seem very basic. Just line up two cars, then 3-2-1 – GO. The first one to the quarter-mile marker wins.

Though the sport may have started that simply, and may still be performed that way in back road challenges, that's not the way it's conducted in the professional ranks. High technology has invaded the sport with starting line time differentials, speeds and elapsed times measured in the thousandths of seconds.

In order to understand what drag racing has become, an examination of a typical dragway (that's what they are usually called) will be instructive.

The cars only race 1320 feet, but the track has to be a lot longer, with room at the start for tire-heating burnouts and staging the cars, and much longer distances at the end of the track to allow the machines to come safely to a stop.

Not all drag strips, however, are a quarter-mile in length. Many are only half that distance (one eighth of a mile), or 'quick drags' as they are sometimes called.

For safety reasons, it's necessary to confine the cars on the track, which is usually done with steel or concrete barriers. Even so, the fans are still quite close to the action on the track.

The track is usually about 30 feet wide for each lane. Lanes are separated by a 'stay-on-your-own-side' white line. Tracks are usually made of blacktop, while the front area of the track, and sometimes a short distance down the track, are made of concrete.

But as the speeds of all classes of drag machines continue to increase by leaps and bounds, consideration for getting the cars stopped becomes of greater importance. Some older tracks are being outmoded because of their short shutdown areas. Many of the national-level tracks use areas of deep sand as a final barrier to slow the cars' last gasps of speed. There are others that have a net at the final end of the area to 'grab' the cars, not unlike the technique used on an aircraft carrier.

A number of turn-off roads allow the drag cars to exit the track surface so that the next pair can begin with minimum delay. Many of the cars will then drive directly back to the pits, though the nitromethane-burning machines are shut down quickly to prevent overheating and are then towed back.

Left: *With large numbers of race entrants, it's imperative to keep things moving along. As the cars leave the starting line, this Norwalk (Ohio) IHRA official signals when the next two cars may begin their burnouts.*

For the experienced drag racer, though, the most important part of the track could be that burnout area. It's also a favorite with the drag fans, as it's the location where the heat, noise, and smoke is generated with great intensity. With the powerful cars of the Pro Classes, the burnouts are simply awe-inspiring.

In order to keep a drag racing show moving along, the cars are lined up in an area called the staging lanes. Then the cars move to the burnout area for their appointed duties.

In the burnout area is a portion of pavement called the water box, where each car rolls through standing water, wetting the tires all the way around. With the dampness reducing the friction between rubber and track, the throttle is then pounded down by the driver and the screaming tires boil up the temperature, resulting in a huge cloud of smoke. The scene is overpowering to sight, sound, and smell.

Below left: *Two Top Alcohol dragsters have just taken the green light and are quickly accelerating down the narrow lanes. The outside retaining walls separate the cars from the spectators, but there is nothing to prevent them from colliding with each other.*

Below: *Full staging lanes ensure continuous action on the track. These cars are awaiting their turn at the 1992 NHRA Spring Nationals.*

Above: *As two Sportsman competitors cross the finish line, the next competitors begin the smoky burnout process.*

Right: *The burnout is just as important at the regional tracks as it is at the national meets. Here, a Kil-Kare Dragway (Ohio) bracket racer torches up the rear rubber.*

Far right: *This Pro Stocker lights up his tires at the 1992 IHRA World Nationals at Norwalk, Ohio. Opinions vary as to the optimum length of the burnout.*

The purpose of this dramatic procedure is two-fold. First, the heated tires are more 'tacky,' and therefore provide more traction. There is also a sticky trail of rubber laid down the track which each driver tries to retrace with his or her run down the track.

At the starting line, no longer is there a brave flagman releasing the cars for their speedy trek down the track. The whole starting procedure revolves around a device located slightly forward of and directly between the cars. The so-called 'Christmas Tree' contains yellow, green and red bulbs, each light having a distinct meaning.

The top yellow stage light indicators are in place for situating the cars on the starting line. There is both a pre-stage and a stage light. When that stage light is illuminated, everything is ready for the run. A special Christmas Tree is used for some Pro Classes, where there is an additional Super Start Light located between the pre-stage and stage positions.

Next comes the flashing of three yellow starting lights, with the bulbs sequencing down the tree together in each lane. This happens if both cars are to leave the line together. But, strangely, that isn't always the case in drag racing today.

In an up-and-coming type of drag racing known as bracket racing, both cars do not necessarily have to leave together, with the time differential coming from the differences in times from earlier runs. It might not look like a fair race from the starting line, but this style of drag racing makes it very close at the finish line.

As might be expected, a green light gets the race started. Of course, to win in this straight line sport, it's necessary to respond as quickly as possible after the green light shines. Most drag racers will tell you that winning and losing is decided right there at the starting line.

Many drivers try to anticipate the light for that near-perfect start. But if a driver is just a split-second too quick on the gas, he'll see the final light on the tree that will end his day. The bottom light, one a driver never hopes to see, is red, and it informs the driver that he's left too soon and is disqualified. Should both cars start too soon, the red light will illuminate for only the first offender. The other driver is permitted to continue.

Once the car has left the starting line, it's timed and exactly 1320 feet later, the timer is shut off. The resulting figure is a car's elapsed time, or ET.

Left: *Once the cars have staged, control of the start of the race belongs to the starter who stands between and behind the cars. As soon as he pushes the button, the cars fill the air with roaring thunder.*

Below: *In drag racing, reaction time at the start is everything. A lead at the start is difficult to overtake, but a driver who leaves too soon is quickly disqualified. There's a fine line between a great start and a red light, as this Sportsman driver has discovered.*

Below: *This is a different perspective of a drag race, viewed from the 'top end' of the strip. Here, two Top Fuelers are completing their runs. The car on the right has broken and shut down, while the nitromethane flames can be seen still emerging from the car on the left.*

One would think that the car with the fastest speed would automatically be the winner, but that is not always the case. A car might have accelerated more quickly during the run, but tailed off at the end of the run. Overall, though, it might be a winner even though its top end speed is lower.

Then too, there's the matter of reaction time at the starting line to consider in the winning equation. The old 'if you snooze, you lose' saying was never more appropriate than in the sport of drag racing. No matter how good a run is made, if a car is left sitting at the green light, the lost distance is very difficult to make up.

The accomplishment of a quick start is appropriately known as a 'hole shot.' Some drivers are masters at getting off the line at almost exactly the same time that the light flashes green. Many top drag racers practice Christmas Trees to keep their reflexes finely tuned.

A tremendous amount of concentration is required to be successful in this sport. Putting that huge power to the pavement at precisely the right split second, keeping the vehicle running straight down the track while not losing traction, and getting across the finish line ahead of the car in the other lane – all of this demands a unique type of mental toughness. You don't have to have bulging muscles to be successful here, but you do have to have excellent coordination, and a bit of a

Above: *With the high speeds achieved by today's drag machines, parachutes are needed to assist in slowing the cars.*

Overleaf: *It only takes a split second for the best of runs with the best of drivers to go awry, as Top Fueler Eddie Hill discovered at Pomona, California in 1989. Air under the front end lifted the car and flipped it over backwards at well over 250 miles per hour. Fortunately, Hill was uninjured.*

Above: *With multiple burnouts and runs down the track, tremendous amounts of rubber become layered on the track surface. Here, an NHRA crew manually heats and scrapes off the excess rubber.*

magic touch. Good eyesight also enters into the drag equation for success. In fact, all the senses have to be tuned to perfection in order to succeed in this sport.

Even experienced superstars such as Don Prudhomme will tell you that you can take nothing for granted even after all his years. On getting a good .start, Don observes, 'With the Top Fuel cars, you have to lift the front a little coming off the line to put the weight on the rear wheels, but you can't overdo it. It's like a teeter-totter. You've got to strike the right balance. Too much too soon and you could lose traction. Everything is happening so quickly that you really have to stay ahead of it.'

It's interesting to watch some of the different pre-staging and staging games that the pro drivers play on each other, as they try to psyche each other out. Some drivers will move into position very slowly, hoping to upset the other driver and cause him possibly to red light.

For most fans, drag racing brings to mind cars duelling it out on the quarter-mile pavement, but

the term also covers a number of other activities which involve beating the other guy from point A to point B.

Drag racing on sand is popular with the off-road set. Two types of off-road drag activities are held: competition on flat ground, and 'uphill drags' where the finish line is considerably higher than the starting line.

The layout of these drag strips is basically the same as their pavement counterparts, though the tracks for the uphill drags are shorter. But there is one major difference that must be taken into account and dealt with between each race. The four wheel drive machines that compete in these races dislodge huge globs of sand or dirt from the starting line. A small 'shovel brigade' rebuilds the course after each run.

There's even drag racing done in the good old gooey mud. This could be the ultimate challenge in the standing-start sport, and the activity draws huge crowds in both indoor and outdoor competitions. The tracks are much shorter than the standard quarter-mile, and runs are often made

Above: *After each pass down the quarter-mile, a car's crew will partially disassemble the motor to check for wear and failed components. Sometimes a complete engine change is required, which results in a frantic effort to get the huge job done in a short time.*

Left: *Track tidiness is the job of the NHRA Safety Safari. This sweeper brushes loose debris from the groove at the starting line. This team is extremely quick at cleaning up an oil spill and making the track raceable in short order.*

singly, with the ET being the determining factor for a winner.

Even the big-tired monster trucks take part in a version of drag racing. The giant trucks have to negotiate several obstacles while trying to beat each other to the finish line. The familiar stacks of cars must be jumped or run over in the course of the race.

There is also a type of drag racing held on the water. This nautical sport rivals the real item in many aspects, with classes of boats which closely resemble those of pavement drag racing. The big difference, though, comes at the start of the race.

Since it's impossible to hold a boat at the line completely dead in the water, the starting technique is slightly different. The engines are started back in the staging area, and the boats approach the starting line together at an idle speed. The green light then flashes and the drivers hammer the throttles. From that point on, it's much the same as standard drag racing.

Right: The procedures for drag racing bikes are identical to those for cars: it's just two-wheeled mayhem instead of four.

Below: Off-road enthusiasts also like drag racing, but here it's done on the dirt. The starting area must be rebuilt after each sand-throwing run.

Above: *Monster trucks also engage in a form of drag racing, only in their case, there's usually several rows of junk cars to jump as well. These trucks normally run much shorter courses than a quarter-mile, and also can perform indoors in arenas.*

Left: *Drag racing on the water adds an extra dimension of danger to this already dangerous sport. These high-powered drag machines must have ideal conditions in terms of wind and the water surface. Eddie Hill is one of the few drivers who has competed in the top classes at the national level on both land and water.*

The Cars

Drag racing offers something for everyone, with great variations in performance, speed and cost for the many types of vehicles which engage in the sport. Pursuit of the sport varies from multi-million dollar teams with national exposure to getting a number painted on the window of the family sedan and pitting it against a neighbor's car on a local track.

Drag racing is a fair endeavor in that equal performance cars race against each other. At first sight, one wonders how all the different types of cars can be classified, but that's exactly what is done. There is a huge number of classes, and this is certainly one of the aspects of drag racing that makes it the exciting sport it is today.

There are many factors that determine a car's class, including whether the engine is carbureted or supercharged, the engine displacement, body style, weight, fuel type and many other factors. The number of classes, and subclasses, seems endless, but there is a logic to the way they are broken down.

The big three classes – Top Fuel, Funny Car and Pro Stock – are considered to be the 'Pro Classes' and, as such, get the lion's share of national media attention and TV exposure. Auto companies provide support to these classes, and successes are flaunted as a part of their national advertising campaigns.

The Top Fuel cars are the top gun machines in the drag racing sport, with their impressive needle-length look and awesome performance. There's certainly no mistaking one of these sleek machines when it's rolled out of its trailer.

About three hundred inches long, the bodies of these cars seem to stretch out to half the length of the track. Aerodynamics are a big factor with these cars, which have a small front wing and a high-mounted rear wing. A Top Fuel car must weigh 1900 pounds, and carries a 500 cubic-inch supercharged engine providing over 4000 horsepower.

Much of the amazing power of these cars is directly related to the nitromethane fuel they use. The nitromethane is mixed with a small amount of methanol to produce the potential for massive power. The power produced by the nitromethane fuel can best be described as a controlled explosion. The tremendous heat and power generated with this fuel is extremely hard on engine components.

Right: The top-gun machines of drag racing have always been the awesome Top Fuel cars. With engines that yield over 4000 horsepower, the machines are capable of speeds in excess of 300 miles per hour, as proven by Kenny Bernstein (seen here) in 1992. Designed for flat-out speed, the cars have reached the astronomical length of 300 inches. Weighing slightly less than a ton, these cars make use of the latest technology, materials, and aerodynamic design.

Left: *The key to the power of both the Top Fuel cars and the Funny Cars is the proper mixing of the nitromethane fuel. Such conditions as altitude, relative humidity, and temperature must be considered. Here, Bruce Larsen checks the specific gravity of the fuel mixture.*

Below left: *To improve aerodynamics and safety, many Top Fuel cars have side pods installed in front of the rear tires. The pods will also collect any blown engine parts and keep them from puncturing the tires.*

Below: *To start one of these high-powered vehicles, you can't just turn the key and step on the gas. Here, a crew member primes a Funny Car's fuel injectors with a shot of starting fluid. The motor is then brought to life by a portable electric starter which is mounted on the blower drive assembly.*

Interestingly, this fuel isn't even a petroleum byproduct. And it's certainly not cheap, going for about $26 a gallon. As many as 15 gallons can be consumed in only one pass. It's dangerous stuff, and during the early days of drag racing it was barred from use. But that's all behind the sport now, as the power generated from this exotic fuel has made the sport as popular as it is today.

As in other types of motorsports, there have been concerns with the increasing speeds of the Top Fuel cars. In 1991, an attempt was made to slow the machines down with a rear end ratio which was far from optimal. But the technological capabilities of the builders and mechanics quickly overcame the restriction, and the speeds and ETs have kept right on climbing.

In March 1992, the first 300 mile per hour run was accomplished, by Kenny Bernstein in Gainesville, Florida. That's about 440 feet per second, or about the length of one and a half football fields.

The powerful cars of the super-popular Funny Car Class have been described as short wheelbase versions of the Top Fuelers. These cars carry a fiberglass stock-appearing body which can be lifted up, hence the nickname 'floppers.' Another big difference in the 2100-pound Funny Cars, which are only slightly slower than the Top Fuelers, is that the 500 cubic-inch powerplant is in front of the driver. This presents the driver with lots of noise, vibration, and danger should there be a fire or explosion.

Top: *For ease of maintenance and inspection between runs, the one-piece Funny Car fiberglass body is removed from the chassis. The operation is extremely easy because of the light weight of the body.*

Above: *You won't find a catalytic converter and muffler on a Funny Car exhaust system! These custom designed and tuned headers are responsible for some of the power generated by the awesome motor.*

Above: *Known as the 'factory racers,' the NHRA Pro Stock cars use stock-appearing bodies and 500 cubic-inch (unlimited in IHRA) normally-aspirated engines. These cars receive significant factory support.*

Like the Top Fuel machines, the Funny Cars also use nitromethane fuel as well as exotic clutches to control the awesome power.

Although their performance approaches that of the Top Fuelers, the look of the Funny Cars is very different. With a 125-inch wheelbase, they are only about a third as long as the Top Fuelers. The bodies roughly resemble their Big Three street counterparts, but they have a more 'squatty' look, with huge rear tires kicking up the rear of the car. The bodies are constructed of either fiberglass or carbon fiber and are extremely light.

In the Pro Stock Class, the nitromethane is put away and regular gasoline is brought out. These cars really do look like passenger cars, with the exception of the large hood scoop. These cars also carry flat rear wings which are nearly

horizontal and protrude far out in the rear.

The NHRA Pro Stocks use 500 cubic-inch powerplants topped with a pair of four-barrel carburetors and produce well over 1000 horsepower. In the IHRA Pro Stock engine rules, unlimited displacement powerplants are legal, resulting in 200 mile per hour, six second quarter-mile performance.

The Pro Stocks are also known as 'factory hot rods,' and since the bodies closely adhere to their showroom counterparts, success on the drag strip gets these cars into national advertising. It should be noted, though, that all Pro Stock cars use rear wheel drive, even though the street versions often are front wheel drive. Somehow, seeing a Pro Stocker doing a burnout with its front wheels just wouldn't be the same.

Left: *The exterior of a Pro Stock car might look factory stock, but the interior is full race with the emphasis on safety. Note the roll cage, seat belts, and driver safety net.*

Below: *With speeds in the 200 mile-per-hour range, it takes more than depressing the brake pedal to stop these machines, as these colorful Pro Stockers demonstrate.*

Established in 1990, the IHRA Pro Mod Class is one of the newest, and most exciting, classes in drag racing. Cars in this class have either a supercharged engine (with a 526 cubic-inch limit) or a nitrous motor (with a 710 cubic-inch limit). These full-bodied cars are capable of six second ETs and 200 mile per hour runs.

Under a wide grouping called the Sportsman category, there are two classes that closely resemble the Top Fuel and Funny Car classes – Top Alcohol Dragster and Top Alcohol Funny Car. With the fuel gulped by these cars being alcohol, the horsepower is reduced considerably, but these machines are still capable of 200+ mile per hour runs.

The Competition Eliminator category (called Modified Eliminator in IHRA) includes just about everything you can imagine. Machines such as supercharged gas coupes, pure dragsters and even full-bodied sedans can fall into this category. Since there's a big difference in performance from car to car, a handicap system is used to equalize the competition. The cars might not start together off the line, but they are really close at the finish.

Below: *Top Alcohol Dragsters look a lot like their Top Fuel big brothers, but looks can be deceiving. Still, these cars turn in a 200+ mph performance in the quarter-mile.*

48

Left: *One of the most popular and innovative classes to be introduced in many years, the IHRA Pro Mod Class rivals the Top Fuel and Funny Car classes for excitement. The motor can either be supercharged or injected with nitrous oxide. Performance is in the 200 mph category, with six second ETs.*

Below: *Top Alcohol Funny Cars are capable of speeds exceeding 200 miles per hour.*

Below: *Just prior to getting the green light, the driver of this Super Comp car will bring the engine revolutions close to the ideal RPMs for the start. As can be seen, the exhaust gates are in the full-open position as the driver prepares for the run.*

Below: *It's sometimes hard to tell the class of a car just by looking at it. This Super Comp car, for example, bears a marked resemblance to a Pro Stock car. The Super Comp's performance , however, is lower than that of the Pro Stocks, running in the 8.90-second category.*

Above: *The NHRA Super Gas and IHRA Super Rod classes specify stock-appearing features with performance not to exceed 9.90 seconds. The interior of this Super Gas car rivals what one might find in the Pro classes.*

Right: *This may look like a mismatch but competition with with dissimilar body styles is the norm in the Super Gas Class. Here, an early British Anglia competes against a late 1960s Chevy Camaro.*

The Super Stock Class, just like in the old days back in the 1960s, uses American production cars with only minor modifications allowed. More than five dozen subclasses exist for both automatic and manual transmission cars.

One important requirement in Super Stock is that the body and motor brand must match. That way, a Ford is really racing a Chevy when they come off the line. That's not to say, though, that you can't use an older engine in a newer body. There is also a handicap system used in this class.

NHRA Super Comp Class (Quick Rod in IHRA) is another category that features a great variety of car styles including production cars, roadsters and gas-burning dragsters. The vehicles can weigh no more than 1300 pounds and be no faster than 8.90 seconds, with handicap starting again the rule.

Right: *This early Vega NHRA Super Street machine pulls a wheelstand coming off the line. Super Street cars must be full-bodied and capable of not better than 10.90 seconds for the quarter-mile.*

Far right: *Bracket racing often pits different styles of cars against each other with a time handicap. Here, the full-bodied car in the far lane has a head start on the old-stlye front-engine dragster in the near lane.*

NHRA Super Gas (Super Rod in IHRA) is a single category for full-bodied cars which must carry doors that open, fenders, grills, a hood, and a windshield. The category features such popular body styles as the Camaro, the Corvette and the Anglia from Britain. The cars must run no faster than 9.90 seconds.

Stock-appearing full-bodied machines are the rule again for the NHRA Super Street Class (Hot Rod in IHRA) which has a 10.90-second index in performance. Like the Super Gas Class, this class requires that cars have all their stock pieces and parts.

The Stock Class has long served as the starting point for many beginning drag racers. Very few changes are allowed, so the cars aren't capable of big performance. This is a place to learn the sport. In this class, aspiring drag racers will bring out their family or personal cars to see what they will do.

Those are the categories and classes for the NHRA/IHRA areas of competition, but on the hundreds of drag strips across the US, different classes of bracket racing are carried out depending on the rules of the particular track. A typical breakout of the classes might be as follows: 0-10.99 seconds, 11.00-12.99 seconds, 13.00-13.99 seconds and 14.00 or slower.

In these classes, drivers are more concerned with running against themselves than with the car in the opposite lane. Here, you make a guess at the speed you will run. Your 'dial-in' speed is then painted on the car glass and the attempt is made to run as close to that speed as possible. Run faster, and you lose! Should the driver in the other lane exceed his time estimate too, the driver who is closest to his guess wins.

Any category of car is eligible to compete in bracket racing, as long as it meets the index times. As such, it's not surprising to see a rail dragster running against a slower full-bodied street car.

The popular drag bike scene also offers many categories of competition. The NHRA Pro Stock

Right: *Every type of
motorsport seems to have
its own special
attractions. In drag racing,
one such example are the
so-called wheelstanders,
which are designed to
perform a wheelstand for
the entire quarter-mile.
One of the most famous
of this breed is Bill
'Maverick' Golden and his
Little Red Wagon.*

Far right: *Top Fuel drag
boats are powered by the
same type of
nitromethane motors that
power Top Fuel cars and
Funny Cars, and run at
nearly 200 mph. If that
speed feels fast on land,
imagine what it feels like
on the water!*

Bike category is reserved for 1981 or newer stock-appearing, carbureted, gas-burning machines. These machines are capable of 7.7-second ETs and speeds of over 170 miles per hour. The Pro Comp Class is capable of speeds of up to 190 miles per hour.

There's also a Funny Bike Top Fuel Class run with another organization, where nitromethane is allowed, unbelievably, on a bike! Quarter-mile times of less than seven seconds and speeds of well over 200 miles per hour are achieved. That kind of performance on two wheels demands very brave men to drive these machines. Like the cars, there are also a number of Sportsman classes for the bikes, including Top Gas (8.20 seconds), Super Comp (8.60 seconds), Pro Gas (9.20 seconds), Super Gas (9.90 seconds), and Super Stock (10.50 seconds). Bikes are also heavily involved in bracket racing.

In the sand drag scene, again there are many classes going all the way from Top Fuel drag-ster down to cars powered by snowmobile engines. Just about every type of vehicle and engine imaginable is put to use. There is also a lot of innovation in the popular mud drag scene, with many different types of vehicles used in competition.

In the drag boat scene, there are many similarities to the 'on land' sport, but the big difference is obviously that the power is not transmitted to a smoking pair of slicks, but to a narrow shaft that leads to a screaming racing prop. Like land drag racing, this sport was also born in California.

Looking at the different boat classes, the Blown Fuel Hydroplanes are the kingpins of the drag boat world. These machines also burn the awesome nitromethane fuel, and have demonstrated speeds of well over 200 miles per hour.

These machines are actually running on a runnel of air created by the forward motion of the hull compressing the air between the sponsons. There is also a Blown Fuel Flatbottom Class and a

Blown Fuel Jet Class, where the machines are powered by a column of water expelled by the same type of unlimited engines, but are somewhat slower than their prop-powered counterparts. Other fuel classes include Unblown Fuel Hydro and Unblown Fuel Flatbottom.

As in their land counterparts, the classes and performance of boat continue to work downward to accommodate many types of vessels. Next, there are blown and unblown alcohol classes before moving to smaller powerplants and pump gas. In the fuel classes, the Chrysler Hemi powerplant is the favorite, with the engines carrying highly modified crankshafts and aluminum blocks. In the smaller unblown classes, the Chevy is the top choice.

Interestingly, the powerplant sits backwards in a drag boat. The exhaust stacks, however, point backward, giving the illusion that the motor is mounted facing forward in the boat. The power is then transmitted forward via a V-drive set-up.

Below right: *Don Garlits, the king of drag racing, has won over 100 NHRA, AHRA, and IHRA events in his long career.*

Far right: *Since an injury caused 'Big Daddy' to retire, Bruce Larsen is now wheeling the latest* Swamp Rat *creation in both NHRA and IHRA competition.*

In the drag racing sport, it's hard to decide who are the real stars – the vehicles themselves, or the drivers who put them through their paces. With the way drag racing has evolved in the 1990s, both enjoy top billing. The drivers have become household names, and their publicity rivals that of any other motorsport.

Here is a look at some of these skilled chauffeurs, both past and present.

Don Garlits – Top Fuel

Mention the sport of drag racing, and the name of 'Big Daddy' Don Garlits comes to mind. Garlits is one of the reasons that drag racing is the big national sport it is today.

Don had 112 victories in his many 'Swamp Rat' machines. Thirty-five wins came in the NHRA, 26 in the IHRA, and 51 with the AHRA organization. He also had 17 Top Fuel championships with all three groups.

Don is known as the master innovator of the sport. It was he who pioneered the rear engine Top Fuel design and the use of the enclosed cockpit. His first victory came in 1956, and his last came exactly 30 years later. The fastest run made

by this living legend was a 287mph/5.07 second blast down the track.

In 1992, Garlits wanted to accomplish the milestone 300 mile per hour run himself, and built a new car for the attempt. Much new technology was introduced, including a canopy-enclosed cockpit, a single-post wing strut, a narrower rear end and a small rear wing. During testing, however, he suffered an eye injury, causing him to announce his retirement.

In recent years, Don has been heavily involved with his drag racing museum in Ocala, Florida. The museum recognizes the pioneers of the drag sport in its Drag Racing Hall of Fame.

Don also serves as a broadcaster on several national networks. What better way to represent drag racing than having 'Big Daddy' explaining the sport!

Left: *Fans of 'Big Daddy' line up to buy souvenirs.*

Shirley Muldowney — Top Fuel

Shirley 'Cha Cha' Muldowney brought female respectability to drag racing, and was one of its most publicized and popular stars during the 1970s and 1980s.

A three-time NHRA Top Fuel Champion (1977, 1980 and 1982), she rates that final championship and the winning of the 1982 US Nationals as the highlights of her illustrious career. She also has 18 career Top Fuel victories and has been in the Top Fuel top ten in points 11 times.

Shirley had a devastating crash in 1984 in which she incurred serious injuries, and didn't return until the 1986 season. She was also the subject of a 1983 movie, 'Heart Like a Wheel,' which detailed her charismatic career.

Below: *Shirley Muldowney blazed a trail for the growing number of women who have followed her in the drag racing sport.*

Connie Kalitta – Top Fuel

Legend Connie Kalitta's three-decade-long career continues into the 1990s. It seems like he's been around forever.

Over the years, his famous 'Bounty Hunter' Top Fuel machines have won seven national NHRA events. In 1962, Connie held the record for the fastest Top Fuel speed, at 180.36 mph. His best results in the NHRA Top Fuel season points were third place finishes in 1982, 1984 and 1985. During the 1970s, Connie also served as crew chief for Shirley Muldowney, and had some very successful years.

He has been joined in the 1990s by son Scott, who will be an able replacement to carry on the family name when Connie finally decides to hang up the gloves.

Don Prudhomme – Top Fuel

Don 'The Snake' Prudhomme has been one of the longtime legends of drag racing. During the 1990s, he shows no signs of slowing down.

Don is best known for his Funny Car activities, and in the 1970s was a four-time NHRA champion (1975 through 1978). He won an amazing seven races during the 1977 season. The Snake was also the first Funny Car pilot to run below six seconds (5.98 seconds) and the first to hit 250 mph, both in 1982. He's been racing since the 1960s and has 35 national Funny Car wins, a national record.

In 1990, he made a big move into the Top Fuel ranks. It was initially not an easy transition, but by his second Top Fuel season he had come up with three wins and four runner-up finishes. His winning trend continued into the 1992 season. Now in his early fifties, The Snake still has a big bite.

Top: *At 50-something, Don Prudhomme has made the transition from Funny Cars, where he won many national championships, to the Top Fuel ranks. Not surprisingly, he has become very competitive in that class also.*

Above: *Don 'The Snake' Prudhomme has brought years of excitement to drag racing, and promises to offer many more.*

Joe Amato – Top Fuel

Joe Amato has been the hottest of the Top Fuel drivers in recent seasons. Always a threat to win, Amato is the only five-time Top Fuel title winner (1984, 1988, 1990, 1991 and 1992). His consistency can be measured by the fact that he has finished second in 1983, 1985, 1987 and 1989. His sparkling career shows no signs of slowing down anytime soon.

Above: *One of the most popular drivers ever to stomp the throttle, handsome Joe Amato has won five NHRA Top Fuel championships.*

Left: *Hot driver Joe Amato has been either first or second in points in nine out of the last ten years.*

Kenny Bernstein – Top Fuel

Another of the top gun Funny Car drivers who made the switch to Top Fuel late in his career, Kenny Bernstein won four NHRA Funny Car titles (1985 through 1988).

In 1990, he made the move to Top Fuel and finished an uncharacteristic eighth in the points. By 1991, he was second in the points.

Then, early in the 1992 season, Kenny did the impossible and set a new standard with a 300 mph run, actually 301.70 mph, at the Gatornationals. He followed it up later in the season with a second 300+ mile per hour run. The accomplishment could well rate as the greatest feat in the straight line sport.

He capped off a phenomenal 1992 season by taking the NHRA championship.

Kenny Bernstein owned 37 national NHRA victories through the 1992 season. His six Top Fuel wins in 1991, in only his second year with those cars, really set the sport on its ear. But those who know Bernstein's driving skills weren't at all surprised.

Besides his many accomplishments on the track, Kenny is one of the most personable drivers in drag racing.

Eddie Hill – Top Fuel

Eddie Hill is one of the most popular drivers in drag racing today. The silver-haired chauffeur is always smiling and amiable with the fans.

He's been racing for nearly four decades, running his first drag race in 1955. In his early drag career, he experienced a number of firsts, including small-profile front tires, charcoal-filled breathers, and smoky burnouts.

In 1965, Eddie moved his drag racing to the water and was a renowned national performer on the scene for many years. In the late 1980s, he returned to NHRA Top Fuel racing and was the first driver to make a four-second run (4.990 seconds in 1988). As of early 1992, he held the national Top Fuel ET record of 4.861 seconds.

Always among the contenders, Eddie's best season finish came in 1988 when he finished third (with four victories). He was fourth in 1987, fifth in 1989, and sixth in both 1990 and 1991. His most hair-raising event took place in 1989, when he was blown over backwards at 270 miles per hour. He was unhurt.

Above: *Kenny Bernstein, who made the first 300 mile-per-hour run in drag racing history, also owns both Indy Car and Winston Cup teams.*

Above: *Eddie Hill has been a favorite with drag racing fans since the 1950s.*

Left: *Here's Eddie in his characteristic yellow Pennzoil Top Fueler doing a burnout at the 1992 NHRA Spring Nationals.*

Ed McCulloch – Top Fuel

Ed 'The Ace' McCulloch ran Funny Cars for over two decades before changing over to Top Fuel in 1992.

He won 18 NHRA Funny Car events and had an outstanding win-loss record of 242-153. He took the prestigious US Nationals five times. As of early 1992, his 5.132-second ET was the fastest Funny Car run ever made. He also ran with IHRA in 1988 and won that group's Funny Car title.

His famous nickname came from a sportswriter in 1965 when he beat a top racer with the nickname 'The King.' The writer wrote, 'The only card higher than a king is an Ace.' He's been known as 'The Ace' ever since.

Above: *Like a number of other top Funny Car drivers, Ed McCulloch also made the move to Top Fuel, where he had several 1992 victories.*

Right: *Young Pat Austin is one of the busiest drag racers in NHRA. He is tough in Top Alcohol Funny Car and Top Fuel competition.*

Pat Austin – Top Fuel

Pat Austin was born to race a drag machine. His career started in Top Alcohol Funny Cars, and through 1991 he had won 43 times. Through 1991, he earned four Top Alcohol national titles.

In 1991, Pat also started driving a Top Fuel machine and even finished 13th in the points that first year. Against unbelievable competition, he also even had a win that year.

Another significant Austin accomplishment took place in 1992, when be became the first Top Fuel driver ever to make a four second run in Canada, with a 4.957-second pass in the NHRA national event in St Pie, Quebec. Pat Austin truly is a star of the future.

Tom Hoover – Funny Car

He's been drag racing for three decades, and 50-something Tom Hoover's Funny Car fires are still burning. His trademark color is black, including his 'Showtime' Funny Car and his clothing.

He started racing in 1962 with all the major racing organizations, and won in all of them. He has also won in Sweden and England.

'I like racing in other countries, where I can help other racers,' he has said. He is as popular over-seas as he is at home.

Hoover ran Top Fuel early in his career, but moved to his present Funny Car mode of trans-portation in 1971. Tom is ably assisted by his 80-something crew chief father. It's easy to see where Tom Hoover gets his spunk and desire!

John Force – Funny Car

Every sport needs a charismatic character, and in drag racing it's the jive-talking Funny Car driver John Force.

More than just talk, Force is the master of the flopper-bodied machines. He won the NHRA title in both 1990 and 1991, was third in 1988, and fourth in 1983, 1986 and 1987.

With the help of longtime crew chief Austin Coil, Force is always the favorite to win. He's famous for his monstrous burnouts, many of which carry past half track. He's also the best at 'backpedal-ing' when the car is losing traction.

Force's career began in 1974, and by 1978 he moved into the national NHRA circuit. Force is a fan favorite, with huge crowds always gathered around his location in the pits.

Top: *The two-generation Hoover Funny Car team has son Tom as the driver and dad George as the crew chief.*

Above: *Mr Excitement, John Force, backs up his bravado with winning action on the track. He's a two-time NHRA Funny Car champion.*

Below: *Bob Glidden is the winningest NHRA driver in history. His forte is the Pro Stock Class, which he has dominated for a decade.*

Right: *The old master, Warren Johnson, really had Pro Stock covered in 1992, when he won his first Pro Stock national title.*

Below: *Great hole shots, super-quick reaction times, and red Fords have long been Bob Glidden trademarks.*

Bob Glidden – Pro Stock

There are a number of terms that are usually associated with Bob Glidden: Winner (first and foremost), Pro Stock, and Ford. He is the longtime king of the 'factory racers.'

Through 1992, Bob had an amazing 80+ wins in NHRA national competition. Add to that the 10 Pro Stock titles he holds, and you get an idea of Bob's predominance. Among his many achievements was the setting of the Pro Stock speed record of 193.21 miles per hour.

He wheeled a Thunderbird between 1983 and 1988 and won an unheard of 39 percent of all the meets he entered. Through 1991, he had qualified first 43 times in his last 103 NHRA events.

Long a family operation, the crew is directed by Bob's wife Etta, and Bob's two sons are crew members. One of the most successful teams in drag racing, Glidden Racing also boasts some of the nicest people in the sport.

Warren Johnson – Pro Stock

That sly old white-haired fox. That's Warren Johnson, one of drag racing's most savvy Pro Stockers.

This Oldsmobile runner is always in the hunt, and in 1992 it finally all came together for him as he took home his first NHRA title. He's been second six times in his long career, the first time in 1976 and the last time in 1991.

The 1991 season was one of his best, with five victories in 11 final rounds. That fabulous season also included the all-time (to that time) quickest ET of 7.180 seconds and a career-best speed of 192.88 miles per hour. The wily Johnson is always looking for the advantage, and in 1991 he fielded a research and development car which was driven by up-and-comer Scott Geoffrion.

There's little doubt that this old pro is going to stick around for even more chances at the NHRA title.

Scott Geoffrion – Pro Stock

Geoffrion showed the Pro Stock boys that he was ready in only his second NHRA Pro Stock season (1991) by finishing fourth.

He rates his victory over superstar Bob Glidden as one of his most memorable moments in drag racing. Scott was also a participant in the quickest Pro Stock race in history, when he lost to 1991 champ Darrell Alderman (7.194 to 7.218 seconds). In 1992, he has become one of the real contenders in Pro Stock.

Jerry Eckman – Pro Stock

Jerry has been drag racing since 1968, when he raced his wife's Camaro at the local drag strip, and he's been going strong ever since.

Eckman ran at the local level until the early 1980s, and in 1983 he made himself known on the NHRA Pro Stock chart for the first time, finishing 16th in the points. He has steadily improved ever since, his best year being 1991 when he was third in the points. He won five events that year, in-

cluding the US Nationals. In all, he's got five national wins.

Eckman has long been considered an excellent qualifier, and wins many of his races thanks to his quick reflexes at the starting line.

Extremely popular with the fans, he's well known by his trademark bright yellow Pennzoil Trans Am racer.

David Schultz – Pro Stock Bike

This is the man to beat in the NHRA Pro Stock Bike class. David Schultz is a three-time national champion (1987, 1988 and 1991), and was the runner-up in 1990. David also won the title with the International Drag Bike Association (IDBA) organization in 1986 and 1989.

His 1991 performance was overwhelming, as he won the first four national events. He has won the NHRA US Nationals three times in his stellar career. Although he started his career on four wheels, driving dragsters, you can bet that it will finish on two wheels.

Above: *Jerry Eckman is a challenging competitor, in his yellow Pennzoil Pontiac Pro Stocker, and is a popular driver with the fans.*

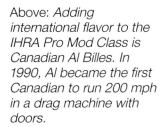

Above: *Adding international flavor to the IHRA Pro Mod Class is Canadian Al Billes. In 1990, Al became the first Canadian to run 200 mph in a drag machine with doors.*

Above right: *Another competitive Canadian with NHRA is Alban Gauthier, who runs in the Pro Stock Class.*

Right: *One of drag racing's growing number of female drivers, Lucinda McFarlin heats the tires of her Pro Stocker at the 1992 US Nationals.*

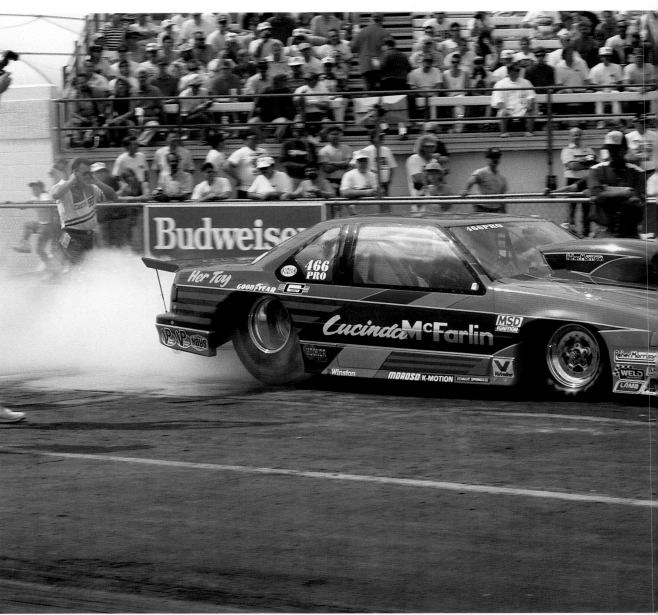

Top: *Shelly Anderson prepares for a run in her Top Alcohol Dragster at the 1992 Spring Nationals at National Trail Dragway near Columbus, Ohio.*

Above: *Known for his long quarter-mile burnouts, British drag racer Norman Wilding carries the British Union Jack into US national drag racing circles.*

The Big Events

The highlights of the drag racing season are the events of the international schedules of the IHRA and NHRA.

In the IHRA, the Spring Nationals, held at Bristol, Tennessee, ran for the 28th time in 1992. Other longtime fan favorites include the US Open Nationals (22 years) and the All-Pro Winter Nationals (20 years), both held at Darlington, South Carolina.

The top IHRA event, though, is the World Nationals, held at Norwalk, Ohio. The 1992 season was the 15th anniversary of this series. The 1992 IHRA slate also showed a trip across the border for the new Summer Nationals at Cayuga Speedway in Toronto, Canada. The NHRA, on the other hand, has been running its LeGrand-national Molson event in Canada for 22 years.

But the pinnacle of the drag sport is the NHRA US Nationals held at Indianapolis Raceway Park. Winning here is like winning the Indy 500 or Daytona 500 in those types of racing.

Right: *The World Nationals at Norwalk, Ohio is IHRA's premier event, held the final weekend in August each year.*

Below: *Hundreds of racers in all classes aspire to make it to the winner's circle against huge odds at the IHRA World Nationals.*

Top: *One of the highlights of the NHRA US Nationals is the Big Bud Shootout, which is worth $50,000 to the winner. Al Hofmann in the BDS car on the far right was the 1992 winner.*

Above: *The top eight drivers in NHRA Funny Car points form the field for the Big Bud Shootout at the US Nationals.*

With over 1000 competitors in all the classes and over 150,000 fans, this is a major event in the world of motorsports. The US Nationals were first held in 1955, and at the time, it was the NHRA's only national event. Many of the other NHRA events have been run for many years and are a must every year for thousands of drag racing fans.

Car clubs across the nation sponsor some of the biggest drag events. During these events, thousands of amateurs bring their machines, often rare examples, to the track to test them. The largest such event is probably the MOPAR Nationals held annually at National Trail Dragway near Columbus, Ohio. Forty thousand fans attended the event in 1992. Other large drag activities include the Buick GS Nationals and a number of Super Chevy car events held every summer. In fact, just about every brand of car has such an activity.

Left: *It doesn't get any louder than this! When two Top Fuelers like Joe Amato and Bruce Larsen mash the gas and light up the tires at the same time, seen here at the 1992 US Nationals, the earth literally shakes from the combined 8000 horsepower.*

Drag racing in the 1990s offers many variations on this popular theme. With the growing fascination for muscle cars of the late 1960s and early 1970s, so-called Muscle Car Shootouts have been instituted. There are other drag events called nostalgia drags, where a car must be of a certain age to enter.

As for the off-road drag events, three national events stand out. The biggest is Gravelrama, held in Cleves, Ohio, which attracts up to 500 competition vehicles each year. Sand-A-Rama in Silver Lake, Michigan, brings out about 250 racers, while 300 show up for the Four Wheel Drive Rodeo in Lisbon, Ohio.

Born and bred in America, drag racing is now moving to all corners of the world. This most basic form of motorsport has become more and more exciting, as new equipment and techniques are developed. It's hard to tell what the future will hold, but there is no doubt that new thrills await fans of drag racing the world over.

NHRA/IHRA Top Class
Drag Racing Records
(Through 1992)

Top Fuel
Elapsed Time

Kenny Bernstein	NHRA	4.792 seconds
Gene Snow	IHRA	4.974 seconds

Top Speed

Kenny Bernstein	NHRA	301.70 miles per hour
Eddie Hill	IHRA	288.55 miles per hour

Funny Car
Elapsed Time

Cruz Pedregon	NHRA	5.076 seconds
Ed McCulloch	IHRA	5.255 seconds

Top Speed

Jim White	NHRA	291.82 miles per hour
Ed McCulloch	IHRA	280.89 miles per hour

Pro Stock
Elapsed Time

Scott Geoffrion	NHRA	7.099 seconds
Billy Huff	IHRA	6.947 seconds

Top Speed

Warren Johnson	NHRA	194.46 miles per hour
Steve Williford	IHRA	205.33 miles per hour

Top Alcohol Funny Car
Elapsed Time

Pat Austin	NHRA	5.853 seconds
Bob Newberry	IHRA	5.951 seconds

Top Speed

Pat Austin	NHRA	240.83 miles per hour
Bob Newberry	IHRA	235.98 miles per hour

Top Alcohol Dragster
Elapsed Time

Chuck Beard	NHRA	5.851 seconds

Top Speed

Roger Odell	NHRA	239.51 miles per hour

Pro Modified
Elapsed Time

Scotty Cannon	IHRA	6.617 seconds

Top Speed

Ed Hoover	IHRA	210.92 miles per hour

Below: *Drag racing is a lot more than speeding in a straight line from point A to point B. The sights, the sounds, the smells, and the speed combine to make drag racing one of the most appealing of all motorsports.*

Drag Strip Directory

ALABAMA

Baileyton Good Time Dragstrip
Baileyton
⅛ mi; Independent

Bama Drag Strip
Jasper
⅛ mi; Independent

Birmington Dragway
Birmington
⅛ mi; IHRA

Chatom Int'l Raceway
Chatom
⅛ mi; IHRA

Green Valley Dragstrip
Gadsden
½ mi; Independent

Huntsville Dragway
Huntsville
⅛ mi; IHRA

Jake's Dragway
Moulton
⅛ mi; Independent

Mobile Int'l Raceway
Irvington
⅛ mi; Independent

Montgomery Int'l Dragway
Montgomery
⅛ mi; Independent

North Alabama Speedway
Tuscumbia
⅛ mi; IHRA

Phenix Dragstrip
Phenix City
⅛ mi; Independent

ALASKA

Polar Raceway Park
Palmer
¼ mi; IHRA

ARIZONA

Firebird Int'l Raceway
Chandler
¼ mi; NHRA

Phoenix Raceway Park
Wittmann
¼ mi; NHRA

ARKANSAS

Centerville Drag Strip
Centerville
1000 ft; Independent

George Ray Hot Rod Drag Strip
Paragould
⅛ mi; Independent

Prescott Raceway Park
Prescott
1000 ft; Independent

CALIFORNIA

Bakersfield Raceway
Bakersfield
¼ mi; NHRA

Carlsbad Raceway
Carlsbad
¼ mi; NHRA

Inyokern Dragstrip
Inyokern
¼ mi; NHRA

Los Angeles County Raceway
Palmdale
¼ mi; NHRA

Pomona Raceway
Pomona
¼ mi; NHRA

Redding Raceway
Redding
¼ mi; NHRA

Sacramento Raceway Park
Sacramento
¼ mi; NHRA

Samoa Airport Dragstrip
Eureka
¼ mi; NHRA

Sears Point Int'l Raceway
Sonoma
¼ mi; NHRA

COLORADO

Bandimere Speedway
Morrison
¼ mi; NHRA

Julesburg Dragway
Julesburg
¼ mi; NHRA

Pueblo Motorsports Park
Pueblo
¼ mi; NHRA

Two Rivers Raceway
Grand Junction
¼ mi; IHRA

DELAWARE

U.S. 13 Dragway
Delmar
¼ mi; NHRA

FLORIDA

Desoto Memorial Dragstrip
Brandenton
¼ mi; NHRA

Gainesville Raceway
Gainesville
¼ mi; NHRA

Jax Raceways
Jacksonville
⅛ mi; NHRA

Miami Hollywood Motorsports Park
Hollywood
¼ mi; NHRA

Moroso Motorsports Park
Palm Beach Gardens
¼ mi; NHRA

Orlando Speed World
Orlando
¼ mi; NHRA

Powerhouse Dragway
Panama City
⅛ mi; NHRA

Sebring Int'l Dragway
Sebring
¼ mi; IHRA

Sunshine Dragway
St. Petersburg
¼ mi; NHRA

GEORGIA

Atlanta Dragway
Commerce
¼ and ⅛ mi; NHRA

Atlanta Speed Shop Dragway
Covington
⅛ mi; IHRA

Brainerd Optimistic Dragstrip
Ringgold
⅛ mi; IHRA

Paradise Drag Strip
Calhoun
⅛ mi; IHRA

Savannah Dragstrip
Savannah
⅛ mi; NHRA

Southeastern Int'l Dragstrip
Dallas
⅛ mi; NHRA

Southern Dragway
Douglas
⅛ mi; NHRA

Twiggs County Dragway
Jeffersonville
⅛ mi; Independent

U.S. 19 Dragway
Albany
⅛ mi; NHRA

Warner Robins Dragway
Warner Robins
⅛ mi; NHRA

HAWAII

Hawaii Raceway Park
Ewia Beach (Oahu)
¼ mi; NHRA

Hilo Dragstrip
Hilo
¼ mi; NHRA

Kauai Raceway Park
Mana (Kauai)
¼ mi; NHRA

Maui Raceway Park
Puunene (Maui)
¼ mi; NHRA

IDAHO

Firebird Raceway
Boise
¼ mi; NHRA

ILLINOIS

Coles County Dragway USA
Charlestown
⅛ mi; NHRA

Cordova Dragway
Cordova
¼ mi; NHRA

Gateway Int'l Raceway
Fairmont City
¼ and ⅛ mi; NHRA

I-57 Dragway
Benton
⅛ mi; IHRA

Mason County Raceway
Havana
⅛ mi; NHRA

INDIANA

Avilla Motor Speedway
Avilla
⅛ mi; IHRA

Brown County Dragway
Nashville
⅛ mi; Independent

Bunker Hill Dragstrip
Kokomo (Bunker Hill)
¼ and ⅛ mi; NHRA

Greater Evansville Raceway
Chandler
⅛ mi; NHRA

Indianapolis Raceway Park
Indianapolis
¼ mi; NHRA

Muncie Dragway
Muncie
¼ mi; IHRA

Osceola Dragway
Osceola
¼ mi; Independent

Speed's Dragway
Freedom (New Hope)
⅛ mi; Independent

Terre Haute Action Track
Terre Haute
⅛ mi; NHRA

IOWA

Cedar Falls Raceway
Cedar Falls
¼ and ⅛ mi; NHRA

Eddyville Dragway
Eddyville
⅛ mi; IHRA

Humboldt County Dragway
Fort Dodge
⅛ mi; IHRA

KANSAS

Great Bend Motorplex
Great Bend
¼ mi; NHRA

Heartland Park Topeka
Topeka
¼ mi; NHRA

Mid-America Dragway
Arkansas City
¼ mi; Independent

Midwest Raceway
Manhattan
⅛ mi; IHRA

Sundown Dragway
Liberal
¼ mi; NHRA

Wichita Int'l Raceway
Wichita
¼ mi; NHRA

KENTUCKY

Beech Bend Raceway
Bowling Green
¼ mi; NHRA

Mountain Motor Speedway
Whitesburg
1/12 mi; IHRA

Mountain Parkway Motorplex
Clay City
¼ mi; IHRA

Ohio Valley Raceway
West Point
⅛ mi; NHRA

River Cities Raceway Park
Ashland
⅛ mi; IHRA

U.S. 60 Raceway
Hardinsburg
⅛ mi; IHRA

Windy Hollow Speedway
Owensboro
⅛ mi; NHRA

LOUISIANA

Louisiana Raceway Park
Eunice
¼ mi; NHRA

State Capital Dragway
Baton Rouge
¼ mi; IHRA

Twin City Dragway
Monroe
¼ mi; NHRA

MAINE

Oxford Plains Speedway
Oxford
⅛ mi; NHRA

Winterport Dragway
Winterport
⅛ mi; NHRA

MARYLAND

Capital Raceway
Crofton
¼ mi; NHRA

Cecil County Dragway
Rising Sun
¼ mi; NHRA

Maryland Int'l Raceway
Budds Creek
¼ mi; IHRA

Mason-Dixon Dragway
Hagerstown
¼ mi; NHRA

75-80 Drag-A-Way
Monrovia
¼ mi; NHRA

U.S. 13 Dragway
Salisbury
¼ mi; NHRA

MICHIGAN

Central Michigan Dragway
Stanton
¼ mi; IHRA

Detroit Dragway
Detroit (Riverview)
¼ mi; NHRA

LaPeer Int'l Dragway
LaPeer
¼ mi; Independent

Milan Int'l Dragway
Milan
¼ mi; IHRA

Northern Michigan Dragway
Kaleva
⅛ mi; NHRA

Ubly Dragway
Ubly
¼ mi; NHRA

U.S. 131 Raceway Park
Martin
¼ mi; NHRA

MINNESOTA

Brainerd Int'l Raceway
Brainerd
¼ mi; NHRA

Grove Creek Speedway
Grove City
⅛ mi; IHRA

Interstate Dragways
Morehead (Glyndon)
¼ mi; NHRA

MISSISSIPPI

Byhalia Raceway Park
Byhalia
⅛ mi; IHRA

Fulton Dragway
Fulton
⅛ mi; Independent

Greenville Dragway
Greenville
¼ mi; NHRA

Gulfport Dragway
Gulfport
¼ mi; Independent

Holly Springs Speedway
Holly Springs
⅛ mi; Independent

Hub City Dragway
Hattiesburg
¼ mi; NHRA

Preston Raceway
Preston
⅛ mi; Independent

MISSOURI

I-55 Raceways
Pevely
⅛ mi; NHRA

Kansas City Int'l Raceway
Kansas City
¼ mi; NHRA

Mid-American Raceway
Wentzville
¼ mi; IHRA

Missouri Int'l Race Park
Benton
¼ mi; NHRA

Mo-Kan Dragway
Ashbury
¼ mi; IHRA

Ozark Int'l Raceway
Rogersville
¼ mi; NHRA

Sikeston Drag Strip
Sikeston
⅛ mi; Independent

U.S. 36 Raceway
Osborn
⅛ mi; IHRA

MONTANA

Lewistown Raceway
Lewistown
¼ mi; NHRA

Lost Creek Raceway
Anaconda
⅛ mi; NHRA

NEBRASKA

Kearney Raceway Park
Kearney
¼ mi; NHRA

Nebraska Motorplex
Scribner
¼ mi; IHRA

NEVADA

Las Vegas Int'l Speedway
Las Vegas
¼ mi; NHRA

NEW HAMPSHIRE

New England Dragway
Epping
¼ mi; IHRA

NEW JERSEY

Atco Raceway
Atco
¼ mi; IHRA

Island Dragway
Great Meadows
¼ mi; NHRA

Old Bridge Township Raceway Park
Englishtown
¼ mi; NHRA

NEW MEXICO

Carlsbad Speedway
Carlsbad
⅛ mi; Independent

The Drag Club
Alamogordo
¼ mi; IHRA

Hobbs Dragway
Hobbs
¼ mi; IHRA

New Mexico Motorsports Dragway
Albuquerque
¼ mi; NHRA

Roswell Dragway
Roswell
¼ mi; NHRA

NEW YORK

Esta Safety Park Dragstrip
Cicero
¼ mi; NHRA

Hampton Dragway
Westhampton
¼ mi; NHRA

Lancaster Speedway
Buffalo
⅛ mi; NHRA

Lebanon Valley Speedway
West Lebanon
¼ mi; NHRA

Long Island Dragway
Long Island
¼ mi

New York Int'l Raceway Park
Leicester
¼ mi; IHRA

Spencer Speedway
Williamson
¹⁄₁₀; IHRA

NORTH CAROLINA
Brewer's Speedway
Rocky Mountain
⅛ mi; Independent

Coastal Plains Dragway
Jacksonville
¼ and ⅛ mi; NHRA

Craven County Dragstrip
Bridgeton
⅛ mi; Independent

Cumberland Int'l Dragway
Fayetteville
⅛ mi; IHRA

Dunn-Benson Dragstrip
Dunn
⅛ mi; IHRA

Farmington Dragway
Winston-Salem
⅛ mi; IHRA

Harrells Raceway
Harrells
⅛ mi; IHRA

Hudson Dragstrip
Hudson
⅛ mi; Independent

Kinston Drag Strip
Kinston
⅛ mi; Independent

McKenzie Race Track
Hollsboro
⅛ mi; NHRA

Mooresville Dragway
Mooresville
⅛ mi; IHRA

North Wilkesboro Dragway
North Wilkesboro
⅛ mi; IHRA

Piedmont Motorsports Park
Greensboro
⅛ mi; NHRA

Rockingham Dragway
Rockingham
¼ mi; NHRA

Rocksboro Dragway
Rocksboro
⅛ mi; IHRA

Shady Side Dragway
Boiling Springs
⅛ mi; Independent

Shuffletown Dragway
Charlotte
⅛ mi; IHRA

Thunder Valley Raceway Park
Red Springs
⅛ mi; Independent

NORTH DAKOTA
Missouri Valley Int'l Raceway
Bismarck
¼ mi; NHRA

OHIO
Dragway 42
West Salem
¼ mi; IHRA

Edgewater Sports Park
Cleves
¼ mi; NHRA

K.D. Dragway
South Webster
⅛ mi; Independent

Kil-Kare Speedway
Xenia
¼ mi; NHRA

Marion City Int'l Raceway
La Rue
¼ mi; IHRA

National Trail Raceway
Newark
¼ mi; NHRA

Norwalk Raceway Park
Norwalk
¼ mi; IHRA

Pacemakers Dragway
Mount Vernon
⅛ mi; NHRA

Quaker City Dragway
Salem
¼ mi; NHRA

Thompson Drag Raceway
Thompson
¼ mi; IHRA

Tri-State Dragway
Hamilton
¼ and ⅛ mi; IHRA

Youngstown Ohio's Drag City
Youngstown
¼ mi; Independent

OKLAHOMA
Ardmore Raceway
Ardmore (Springer)
¼ mi; NHRA

Thunder Valley Raceway Park
Norman
¼ mi; NHRA

Tulsa Int'l Raceway
Tulsa
¼ mi; NHRA

OREGON
Coos Bay Int'l Speedway
Coos Bay
¼ mi; NHRA

Jackson County Sports Park
Medford
¼ mi; NHRA

Madras Raceway Park
Madras
⅛ mi; NHRA

Portland Int'l Raceway
Portland
⅛ mi; NHRA

Woodburn Dragstrip
Woodburn
¼ mi; NHRA

PENNSYLVANIA
Beaver Springs Dragway
Beaver Springs
¼ mi; NHRA

Keystone Raceway Park
New Alexandria
¼ mi; NHRA

Maple Grove Raceway
Mohnton
¼ mi; NHRA

Numidia Raceway
Bloomsburg
¼ mi; NHRA

South Mountain Dragway
Boiling Springs
⅛ mi; NHRA

Sunset Drag Strip
Hermitage
¹⁄₁₀ mi; Independent

SOUTH CAROLINA
Carolina Dragway
Jackson
¼ mi; Independent

Cooper River Dragstrip
Summerville
⅛ mi; Independent

Darlington Int'l Dragway
Darlington
¼ mi; IHRA

Dorchester Dragway
Dorchester
⅛ mi; IHRA

Florence-Darlington Dragstrip
Florence
⅛ mi; IHRA

Greer Dragway
Greer
⅛ mi; IHRA

North Myrtle Beach Dragstrip
North Myrtle Beach
⅛ mi; Independent

Orangeburg Drag Strip
Orangeburg
⅛ mi; IHRA

Ware Shoals Dragway
Ware Shoals
⅛ mi; IHRA

SOUTH DAKOTA
Dakota Intermountain Dragway
Belle Fourche
¼ mi; NHRA

Thunder Valley Dragway
Marion
¼ mi; NHRA

TENNESSEE
Bristol Int'l Dragway
Bristol
¼ mi; IHRA

Cherokee Dragway
Rogersville
⅛ mi; IHRA

Clarksville Speedway
Clarksville
⅛ mi; IHRA

Four-Eleven (411) Motor Speedway
Knoxville
⅛ mi; IHRA

I-40 Dragway
Crossville
⅛ mi; IHRA

Jackson Dragway
Jackson
⅛ mi; IHRA

Knoxville Dragway
Knoxville
⅛ mi; IHRA

Memphis Motorsports Park
Memphis
¼ mi; NHRA

Middle Tennessee Dragway
Cookeville
⅛ mi; IHRA

Music City Raceway
Nashville (Union Hill)
⅛ mi; NHRA

Riverside Raceway Park
Nashville
¼ mi; IHRA

TEXAS
Alamo Dragway
San Antonio
¼ mi; IHRA

Amarillo Dragway
Amarillo
¼ mi; NHRA

Big Valley Raceway
Edinburg
¼ mi; NHRA

Cedar Creek Dragway
Kemp
⅛ mi; Independent

Eastex Dragway
Houston (Porter)
⅛ mi; NHRA

El Paso Dragway
El Paso
¼ mi; NHRA

Hallsville Raceway
Longview (Hallsville)
¼ mi; NHRA

Houston Raceway Park
Baytown
¼ mi; NHRA

Idalou Motorsports
Lubbock
¼ mi; IHRA

Paris Drag Strip
Paris
1000 ft; NHRA

Penwell Raceway
Odessa (Penwell)
¼ mi; IHRA

Temple Academy Dragway
Temple
¼ mi; Independent

Texas Motorplex
Ennis
¼ mi; NHRA

Texas Raceway
Fort Worth (Kennedale)
⅛ mi; NHRA

Valley Dragway
San Angelo (Wall)
¼ mi; Independent

Wichita Falls Dragstrip
Wichita Falls
⅛ mi; NHRA

UTAH
Bonneville Raceway Park
Salt Lake City
¼ mi; NHRA

Dixie Raceway
St. George
¼ mi; Independent

Grand Valley Dragstrip
Moab
¼ mi; NHRA

VIRGINIA
Big Al's Dragway
Richlands (Cedar Bluff)
⅛ mi; IHRA

Colonial Beach Dragway
Colonial Beach
⅛ mi; IHRA

Eastside Speedway
Waynesboro
⅛ mi; IHRA

Elk Creek Dragway
Elk Creek
⅛ mi; IHRA

New London Dragstrip
Lynchburg
⅛ mi; IHRA

Old Dominion Speedway
Manassas
⅛ mi; IHRA

Richmond Dragway
Richmond
¼ mi; IHRA

Suffolk Raceway
Lynchburg
¼ mi; IHRA

Sumerduck Dragway
Culpeper
⅛ mi; NHRA

WASHINGTON
Bremerton Raceway
Bremerton
¼ mi; NHRA

Renegade Raceway
Yakima
¼ mi; NHRA

Seattle Int'l Raceway
Kent
¼ mi; NHRA

Spokane Raceway Park
Spokane
¼ mi; AHRA

WEST VIRGINIA
Fairmont Dragway
Fairmont
⅛ mi; NHRA

Fastway Motorsports Park
Burlington
⅛ mi; Independent

Grandview Dragway
Beckley
⅛ mi; IHRA

Princeton Speedway
Princeton
⅛ mi; IHRA

WISCONSIN
Great Lakes Dragway
Union Grove
¼ mi; NHRA

Rock Falls Raceway
Eau Claire
¼ mi; NHRA

Wisconsin Int'l Raceway
Kaukauna
¼ mi; IHRA

WYOMING
Douglas Int'l Raceway
Douglas
¼ mi; NHRA

CANADA
ALBERTA
Capital City Raceway Park
Edmonton
¼ mi; NHRA

MHBRA Raceway
Medicine Hat
⅛ mi; NHRA

Race City Speedway
Calgary
¼ mi; NHRA

BRITISH COLUMBIA
Eagle Motorplex
Cache Creek
¼ mi; NHRA

Kelowna Motor and Sport Park
Kelowna
⅛ mi; Independent

Mission Raceway
Mission
¼ mi; Independent

North Central Raceway Park
Prince George
¼ mi; Independent

Western Speedway
Victoria
¼ mi; Independent

MANITOBA
Dragways International
Gimli
¼ mi; NHRA

NEW BRUNSWICK
Pennfield Int'l Dragway
Pennfield
¼ mi; NHRA

NOVA SCOTIA
Maitland Dragway
Maitland
¼ mi; NHRA

ONTARIO
Cayuga Motorsports Park
Cayuga
¼ mi; IHRA

London Motorsports Park
St Thomas
¼ mi; NHRA

Shannonville Motorsports Park
Belleville
¼ mi; CASC/RACE

PRINCE EDWARD ISLAND
Raceway Park
Charlottetown
¼ mi; NHRA

QUEBEC
Autodrome St-Eustache
St Eustache
⅛ mi; Independent

Autodrome St-Felicien
St Felicien
¼ mi; Independent

Luskville Dragway
Aylmer
¼ mi; NHRA

Napierville Dragway
Napierville
¼ mi; NHRA

Piste D'Acceleration Pont Rouge
Pont Rouge
¼ mi; NHRA

Sanair Super Speedway
St Pie
¼ mi; NHRA

SASKATCHEWAN
Saskatchewan Int'l Raceway
Saskatoon
¼ mi; NHRA

MEXICO
Autodromo De Monterrey
Guadalupe
¼ mi

GREAT BRITAIN
BEDFORDSHIRE
Santa Pod Dragway
¼ mi

STRATFORDSHIRE
Avon Park Raceway
Stratford-Upon-Avon
¼ mi

YORKSHIRE
York Dragway
Melbourne
¼ mi

Index

80